To Marika & [W...]

You are so ble[ssed]

have such a wonderful [dad]

& mom. I've known your dad for

many years. He's an amazing

guy & one was the fastest

on the planet!

Grace & peace,

Cary Kno[...]

Eph. 2:8-9 &

3-20-21

Presented to:

_____

By:

_____

Kids Talk About God ™

Carey Kinsolving and Friends

www.kidstalkaboutgod.com

Kids Talk About God™

6

Miller,

If God gave you unlimited power for one day, what three things would you do?

I would change my dog into a cat. I would change my bird into a sister. I would like for my grandparents to come back from out of town.

Hanah, 6

I would slide down a rainbow. I would have a new baby brother. I would get a lizard.

Rebekah, 6

I would make summer last forever because that's the only season I like.

Vicki, 11

I would clear the world of litter and sin. Then, I would make everyone like Jesus.

Andrew, 8

I would like to fly. I want to touch the sun. I want to fly past my house.

Michael, 6

I would give my mom whatever she really wanted. I would give my dad $100.

Kristin, 8

7

What color is

God is a rainbow color because He loves all people.

Hunter, 7

God is green and blue because the earth is green and blue.

Zack, 8

I think God is light blue and white because I think He watches us from the clouds.

Brittany, 9

God is gray because He is very powerful.

Patrick, 8

I think God is gold because He shines over us, and He helps us be kind and merciful to others.

Lindsay, 7

God?

Curt, 10

9

10

Why did God make us?

I think God made us because He wanted to see somebody playing and having fun.

Sara, 8

God made us because He was tired of seeing dinosaurs on the world.

Austin, 7

God made us because He was bored of just sitting up in heaven looking down at nothing.

Jordan, 10

I think God created us because He thought we would be special, and it turns out we are special!

Chelsea, 8

God wanted somebody to love Him, to trust Him, to know about Him, and He was finding somebody to love.

Gina, 7

Carl, 9

11

We cannot see God because He needs His privacy.

Patrick, 10

God likes to be alone. If everybody saw Him, they would always crowd around Him.

Megan, 8

God is spirit. You believe in God like you would believe in air. You cannot see it, but you know it is there.

Andrew, 11

I really want to know what God looks like. I can't wait to meet my maker!

Elizabeth, 12

God?

We can't see
God because
man is a sinner.
God is perfect,
and a sinner and
God don't mix.

William, 12

Ashby, 9

13

We are all children of God.

Gloria, 7

Why did God make people different from each other?

We have to have people who want to do all sorts of things and work at different jobs. Little odd jobs are very important.

Leslie, 12

It is so much more fun this way, and God knows that.

Nicole, 9

The world would be so plain if everyone was the same.

Amanda, 10

So He wouldn't be bored.

Michael, 7

God wanted to show His ability to be creative by making every color.

Andy, 12

15

Who wrote the

God wrote the Bible because He wanted us to know Him and what He did for us.

Nicole, 9

God thought up the Bible, but He gave people the mind to write the Bible.

Anna, 9

I think the angels wrote the verses, and God helped the angels type it out.

Sara, 8

Some names of some people are Matthew, Mark, Luke and John, and if they misspelled a word, then they would have to start over.

Jennifer, 9

I think the disciples wrote it, and Jesus and God. They wrote it on scrolls. Then they cut it in squares, and they got leather and made the cover and put it together.

Robert, 8

16

Sam, 6

What

Mary, 8

s God's favorite food in heaven?

God's favorite food is bread because He saved the Israelites with manna (a kind of bread).

Emily, 12

God does not have a favorite food because He doesn't eat because He is always watching over us.

Philip, 12

God's favorite food is goldfish because the streets of heaven are paved with gold.

Kate, 6

The fruit that was growing on the tree in the middle of the Garden of Eden.

Laia, 14

What is the lesson of Moses and the children of Israel's crossing the Red Sea?

It means to me that no false god can overcome the true God.

Michael, 10

The lesson is, if you need the Lord's help, call upon Him and He will help you.

Amber, 11

Trust in the Lord even when you are scared.

Shannon, 11

If you trust God, He will help you in sticky situations.

Rachel, 11

Britni, 7

20

21

Rachel, 7

What is God's favorite song?

God doesn't like any particular song. He loves them ALL!

Michael, 12

"If Loving God Was a Crime, I'd Be an Outlaw" is God's favorite song.

Ross, 11

God's favorite song is the Hallelujah Chorus because hallelujah means "praise to God."

Marissa, 11

God likes every song that praises Him.

Amanda, 11

God's favorite song is "Jesus Loves the Little Children."

Martha, 8

23

In the Garden of Eden, why did the devil tempt Eve instead of Adam?

Because Satan is a boy and boys don't like girls.

Rachel, 9

Eve forgot they weren't supposed to eat that tree, and then Adam forgot.

Nicole, 8

Eve hadn't lived there as long as Adam.

Katie, 11

Eve was just walking around, and I think Adam was busy.

Victoria, 8

Eve was more sensitive than Adam.

Clay, 9

She was in the wrong place at the wrong time.

Megan, 10

24

25

Carey Ann, 1

Which of the Ten Commandments is the most important?

The first one is the most important, because the Lord is our God, and if He wasn't, we wouldn't be here.

Laura, 9

Honoring your parents is especially important because if you don't, it will get you into trouble.

Alyssa, 8

"You shall have no other gods before me." because if you don't believe in God, why should you worry about following all the other commandments?

Nathan, 10

If you did not obey your mom and dad, they would stay mad at you, and God would not like that.

Taylor, 10

"You shall not lie" is the most important because you can get someone else into trouble.

Laura, 7

How

I think you
know God
loves you
because
He died
for us.

Jordan, 10

Brooke, 9

28

o you know God loves you?

I can see flowers,
I can taste cake,
I can hear birds,
I can feel my cat,
and I can smell
the flowers!

Sikas, 9

God made me so
that I could run,
jump, and play. He
gave me a very
lovable and
obedient dog.

Megan, 9

I know God loves
me because He gave
me a smart mind.

Chris, 9

I know God loves me because He helps me with my
requests and answers all my prayers.

Alex, 11

29

What is the lesson of Daniel in the lion's den?

The lesson is to pray always and to forgive people.

Taylor, 6

It teaches me that God is going to fix all of my problems, even the ones that I think will "eat me up!"

Hillary, 10

You should always pray to God, even if you will be punished.

Andrew, 8

The lesson is to keep your mouth shut and to trust in God in every way and every day.

Elizabeth, 11

30

Andrew, 9

AAA!

Why does God allow bad things to happen to people?

God wants us to ask Him for help.

Katherine, 7

God uses bad things as wake-up calls to get our attention so we realize He is in control.

Russell, 9

God wants us to believe in Him so that we will have faith.

Rachel, 9

...is DOG is full of JUICE!

We deserved to be punished for our sins, but remember that God suffered worse.

Launa, 8

What would it be like if Adam and Eve hadn't eaten the forbidden fruit?

Bees wouldn't sting, bears wouldn't bite, and bad things wouldn't happen.

Amanda, 6

We would be having fun and worshipping God.

Kelly, 9

There would be no homeless people or people that live in the streets or unhealthy people.

Kyle, 9

God would walk with us.

Chris, 11

You could keep lions and tigers for pets.

Marci, 9

He is our Light

Juliet, 11

What is God like?

God is cool, awesome, powerful, nice, big, huge, wonderful, loving, exciting, caring, giving and The Best!

Adrienne, 8

God is very loving. I imagine He is very tall. I love Him.

Lauren, 9

God is like an apple. Apples look good on the outside and on the inside.

Brandon, 10

God has big hands because He's got the whole world in His hands.

Kalen, 9

God is like a never-ending story that you want to read again and again.

Ashley, 10

I think he has a beard. He is not that old. He lives in heaven. Jesus is His son.

Justin, 10

37

How can God be everywhere?

God can be everywhere because He is bigger than the world.

Shelby, 7

God is powerful, and He loves us, so He always wants to be around us all the time.

Katherine, 10

God can be everywhere because, well, He's God.

Owen, 9

God can be everywhere because He wants to be close to us.

Bethany, 7

God has angels everywhere to help Him be everywhere.

Emilee, 8

Megan, 8

Why did God command us not to covet?

God wants you to find happiness in what you have.

Kendal, 11

God told us not to covet because He will provide us with what we mostly need, not junk that we don't even use.

Christine, 11

Because sometimes if you can't get it out of your head, it might bug you.

Avery, 8

If everyone in the whole world coveted, there would be no peace nor kindness throughout the world.

Sika, 9

Teddy, 10

Why do we sin?

Sin is a bad habit that just comes naturally.

Leslie, 12

We are born with a want to sin.

Taylor, 9

We sin because we don't listen.

Michael, 6

Adam and Eve started the sinning generation.

Drew, 10

Adam and Eve messed up so we are born with sin in our hearts.

Dominique, 6

We sin to get out of things.

Lynden, 8

Bradley, 10

Do babies go to heaven when they die?

Babies go to heaven because they are not old enough to understand sin, Jesus Christ, and the Holy Spirit.

Molly, 12

Babies go to heaven because that's where they belong.

Kelly, 6

My baby cousin died and went to heaven. She gets to see God every day, and just think about the wonderful toys she gets to play with. Even though I'm sad, I know Martha Caroline is the sweetest little angel in heaven.

Hillary, 9

44

God loves babyis

Joy in heaven

Joy in heaven

Joy in heaven

God loves babyis

God loves babyis

Joy in heaven

Elizabeth, 8

45

46

What is the lesson of Noah and the Ark?

Even if people doubt you and say you're crazy, just ignore them. Remember, you're doing it for God.

Brittany, 11

Don't fail to believe before it's too late.

Richard, 13

Everyone except Noah was wicked. He probably had a lot of peer pressure.

Maria, 11

Always prepare for things that are coming up.

Brian, 10

Don't laugh at your neighbor cause they might be right.

Rebekah, 10

Kassie, 6

47

How would the angels announce Jesus' birth today?

The angels would go door-to-door and tell each family: "Don't be afraid. Come and see!"

Carson, 6

I think the angel would tell Mrs. Higgy. She is the children's choir and song director. She is also the costume person for all the plays.

Jordon, 9

The angel might appear before homeless people because they are not rich, important people. The angel might say Jesus had been born in a shack, a tent, or an apartment.

Maria, 12

Homeless She

Nolan, 9

50

John, 8

How did the wise men know about Jesus' birth?

Maybe the wise men were friends of Joseph.

Joseph, 6

That's why they were called wise men!

Ellen, 6

It was the Star of David in the sky.

Drew, 11

They saw a different star. They just knew that since there was a new star there must be something special.

Elizabeth, 7

51

If you
wise
would

I would bring a
dog to Jesus
because He neede
protection.

Hunter, 6

Kelsey, 7

were one of the men, what gifts you bring to Jesus?

I would give Jesus a lot of money, a big sheep, and a balloon that reads, "It's a boy!"

Perry, 11

I would bring my heart. That's all Jesus needs from me.

Jackie, 9

I would give Him as much gold as I could find, but I can't give Him anything to pay Him for dying for me.

Kevin, 10

I would bring Him a friend because friends are fun to play with.

Laurie, 7

EXplain God.

One of God's main jobs is making people. He makes them to replace the ones who die so there will be enough people to take care of things here on earth. He doesn't make grown-ups, just babies. I think they are smaller and easier to make. That way He doesn't have to take up His valuable time teaching them to walk and talk. He can just leave that to the mothers and fathers.

God's second-most important job is listening to prayers. An awful lot of this goes on since some people, like preachers and things, pray at times besides bedtime. God doesn't have time to listen to the radio or TV on account of this. Since He hears everything, not only prayers, there must be a terrible lot of noise in His ears unless He has thought of a way to turn it off.

God sees everything and hears everything and is every-where, which keeps Him pretty busy. So you shouldn't go wasting His time by going over your parents' head and asking for something they said you couldn't have.

Danny, 8

55

Why does the Bible say, "Honor your father and mother"?

I honor my parents by giving them hugs and kisses. I also honor them by buying them TCBY treats.

Angela, 10

I honor my parents by obeying. Like when they say to get them some water, I do it. I treat them like a king and queen.

Christine, 10

I obey my mother and father by getting up in the mornings as sweet as pie.

Kaitlin, 7

I love my mother and father. They are the best. I try to obey them. I know they love me, and I love them.

Gardner, 11

Ryan, 12

57

Rainey, 10

How do you know God hears you when you pray?

I know because I prayed for my grandmother. She has a rare type of cancer, and God has kept her alive for 13 years.

Deana, 10

If you ask for candy but if you don't need it, God might not give it to you. If you pray for safety, He will give you safety.

Whitney, 10

One time I prayed for my brother to get well, and the next day he was healed.

Paul, 9

God will answer you, but it might not be what you expected.

James, 11

60

If you are a Christian and you sin, can you go to heaven?

Yes, once you are in God's hands, no one can pluck you out.

Tyler, 12

If you are a Christian, you will go to heaven. God is in your heart, and He won't leave.

Austin, 9

Yes, I will go to heaven with my grandfather.

Austin, 7

61

Brittain, 12

Why did Jesus tell Peter to go to the sea to find a coin in the mouth of a fish?

Jesus didn't want to hurt the feelings of the tax collectors.

Sam, 7

I don't know why Jesus told Peter to find the coin in the mouth of a fish. Maybe He likes fish.

Barrett, 12

Because He wanted to pay His temple tax and Peter's.

Kendall, 12

62

Allison, 11

63

What did Jesus mean when He said, "I am the bread of life"?

Jesus meant I am the bread, and you are the butter as in "I am in charge of you."

Elisabeth, 9

Jesus meant you will never go hungry.

Kristin, 6

Jesus meant we should crave Him like we crave food or bread.

Denise, 11

Jesus meant that if you listened to Him or lived off His word that you would have everlasting life.

Rainey, 10

Katie, 9

= Everlasting Life

"I'm A Miracle

66

Why does God perform miracles?

God performed miracles because people needed them.

Ryan, 8

God performed miracles because Jesus would not be on this earth if God hadn't performed miracles.

Jerra, 7

God performed miracles so people would know that He was the Messiah and to help people.

Julie 10

Jennifer, 10

Because God has been prepari[ng] a place for them heaven.

Molly, 8

Matt, 9

68

Why do people have to die?

The reason people die is so we can go to heaven and watch over our loved ones.

Tiffany, 9

Earth is just a place for us to get ready for heaven. Maybe some people are ready to go to heaven before others.

Ben, 9

I really don't know why some people die before others, but the important thing is not what age you are when you die; it's whether Jesus lives in your heart. If He does, you will live with Him in heaven forever.

Rainey, 10

God's Will

Your Will

So He could have people on His side.

Damian, 9

70

Julie, 10

Why did God give us a choice between spiritual life and spiritual death?

God gave us a choice so we can do what we want with our life.

Kristin, 9

God wanted to test what He made.

Cory, 9

God gave us a choice because He didn't want to force everyone to love Him.

Mariah, 8

God wanted to see if we loved Him enough to choose to live with Him.

Shelby, 10

Johnny, 12

Why did Peter deny Jesus three times?

Peter was weak.

Kyle, 6

Peter denied Jesus three times because he forgot that he had power in God.

Dominique, 6

He forgot that God was in control.

Raha, 7

Peter forgot to have faith in Jesus.

Kelsey, 7

What does Easter mean to you?

Easter is really a pagan holiday with all the bunnies and chicks. But if you celebrate in the right way about Jesus, it is a good holiday.

Hannah, 9

Easter is when Jesus was resurrected, and when the Easter bunny comes to see us the night before.

Mason, 11

God is the greatest person in the universe. He died for our sins and for us so we could be saved.

Kendall, 11

Easter means God has risen from the dead and was walking around the city and went to talk to the disciples and went back to heaven.

Marce, 11

74

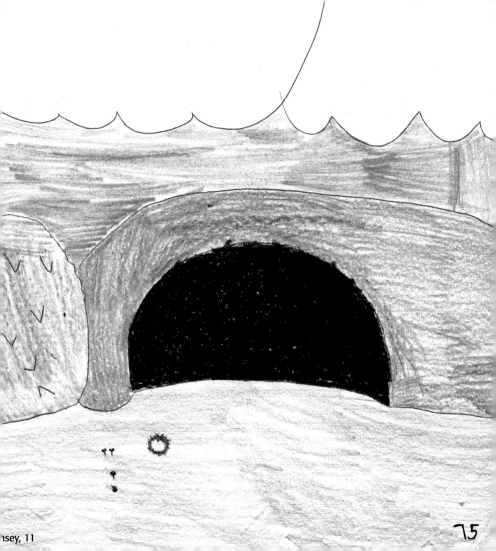

75

How
that

Bethany, 11

do I know for sure I'm doing what God wants me to do?

You're doing something wrong, the Holy Spirit will convict you.

Jannae, 9

I am reading the Bible and praying.

Corine, 6

I'm doing good and doing what Mom and Dad tell me to do.

Ethen, 6

If you don't want to tell your parents, it's not what God wants you to do.

Lacey, 12

The Bible is a gold-
mine for learning right
from wrong

James, 12

How does the Holy Spirit convict us of sin?

If you have Jesus in your heart, the Holy Spirit will tell you what God's will is.

Shelby, 10

I can hear Him in my mind when nobody is around me.

Grace, 8

Your heart feels sad, and you feel like you need to talk to God.

Jen, 12

The Bible is God's special instruction book for you to read and check your progress.

Heather, 12

He tells us in our sleep.

Morgan, 7

79

What is wisdom, and who is the wisest person you know?

My mother is wise because she gave me good advice to check my work, and boy does it work!

Ashley, 9

The wisest person I know is my mom because she has helped me and my big sister with a lot of stuff and mostly all the things were right.

Sarah, 9

The wisest person I know is Jesus. He died on the cross for our sins.

Melissa, 10

I think someone who asks for wisdom is wise.

Mandy, 11

The Fear Of The Lord
Is The Beginning Of
Wisdom.

Proverbs 9:10

King Solomon

81

Ariel, 7

Who is the greatest in the kingdom of heaven?

Children!

Kelley, 6

A servant will be great in heaven, next to God.

Philip, 12

Whoever humbles himself like a little child is greatest in the kingdom of heaven.

Daniel, 11

How powerful is God?

God is so powerful He can be the best pilot in the Navy.

Zach, 7

God could carry 1 million blue whales on His finger.

Carter, 10

God is so powerful He can take away our sin.

Katy, 7

God is so powerful He could split the sun in half and make a friendship necklace.

Dominique, 6

God is so powerful, He can burn water!

Geoffrey, 8

God has love in His power.

Lindsay, 6

Max, 7

85

David AND Goliath

What is the lesson of David and Goliath?

If you're going to wear armor, ask God for the armor.

Michael, 11

Pick on someone your own size.

Melissa, 9

Big people don't get to do all the big things. If we believe in God, we can do anything.

Sarah, 10

Never underestimate the power of God or a boy.

Philip, 11

Size doesn't matter. It's your faith in God.

Rachel, 10

Jason, 11

Why does God let Us sin?

We have free will to choose to do good or bad. I like free will.

Paul, 10

God must not want robots.

Josh, 12

God gives choices. Not necessarily to sin, but to make choices for Him.

Taylor, 11

God wants us to do good for Him with love, not because He made us do it.

Austin, 10

God doesn't let us sin. We have a want to sin.

Laura, 9

Will, 9

In the ninth commandment, why did God command us not to lie?

The problem with lying is that once you start, it's hard to stop.

Aaron, 9

If you broke something, and you said your baby sister did it, you would get into some serious trouble.

Emile, 8

When you tell the truth, you feel good about yourself. And when you lie, you don't feel good.

Nicole, 9

Lying makes God sad.

Kassie, 6

Lying can cause great confusion among everyone.

Meg, 11

WhY

So they can watch over us and be our garden angels.

Lauren, 9

Mary, 9

o angels have wings?

So they can be guardians for us even when we are in cars and on roller coasters!

Hillary, 11

So they can fly on top of you and watch over you without having to sit on you.

Lauren, 11

Angels have wings so they can fly down and when babies are born, they can bless them.

John, 6

God put wings on angels so they can stay in heaven and not fall on the ground.

Britni, 10

93

How can I tell what's right from what's wrong?

You can really tell right from wrong because there is this little thing inside you that bothers you a whole bunch when you tell a lie or something like that.

Dave, 10

If you think your mom wouldn't let you do it, then you shouldn't do it.

Nicole, 10

The heart pumps fast when you are doing wrong and pumps slow when you are doing good.

Taylor, 10

If you follow the 10 commandments, you are doing right. But if you break them, you are doing wrong.

Taylor, 10

When I start to do something wrong, I feel like I have a stomachache.

Scott, 10

od made Addm and Eve.

satan 'tempted Eve.

Adam sinned against God.

The guarding angel.

exander, 8

95

"Differing weights and differing measures— the Lord detests them both."

Jennifer, 10

WHY did God command us not to steal?

When people steal, their conscience bothers them.

Beth, 10

Stealing is just plain mean.

Heather, 10

We should not steal because we didn't work for it. The other person worked for it.

Lee, 9

If you think nobody saw you, think again because God sees everything you do.

Casey, 10

God wants us to be happy with what we have.

Nathan 11

98

What can we take to heaven?

I'll pack my toothbrush and toothpaste, my blanket and my stuffed animal.

Nicole, 8

We can't take anything to heaven with us because we won't need anything in heaven besides what's already there. God is there, and He is all that anyone needs.

Emily, 12

You can take your spirit and you will leave your old body. You will get a new body in heaven.

Natalie, 9

I will take a loving heart.

Adam, 10

God will be my treasure when I get to heaven!

Jamie, 11

ek, 8

99

JESUS CALMS THE SEA

100

Anna, 7

How can Jesus be 100 percent God and 100 percent man?

Jesus had to die on the cross in man form, and He lived in the heavens.

Annastasia, 8

Anything is possible for God.

Donald, 12

He's the Son of God first. Then, when He was born on earth, He became the Son of Man, too.

Stefanie, 12

God sent Jesus to live in a body on earth, so He was man and God at once.

Rachel, 8

He did things like His dad (100 percent God!) and He did things like we do (since He's 100 percent man!).

Candice, 10

Kathleen, 11

How does God talk to you?

God used to talk out loud so that people could hear Him like any other person. Now He doesn't do that. He talks to us through our hearts.

Hannah, 9

God puts it in your heart, and it goes all the way to your brain.

Taylor, 6

I think the way God talks to us is through the Bible, but we must read and study it.

Kyle, 12

When you pray to God, and you're very still and quiet, you can hear Him.

Hillary, 6

God can talk by thunder because thunder is really God talking out loud.

Dianna, 8

104

What does God do?

God sends guardian angels to watch over us. God tells us what's right and what's wrong. He also protects us. Most of all, He loves us.

Tiffany, 10

God does almost everything. He watches us while we're asleep, and He watches us in the day, too. He never sleeps, and He never gets hurt. But the most important thing is He never lets us down.

Caleb, 10

God sits on his throne. He forgives people. He listens to people's prayers. And He loves everyone.

Trent, 10

God teaches, performs miracles, creates, keeps the Devil away from us, loves, gives, saves, and speaks. God and angels bowl, and God rests.

Hannah, 9

God helps people with problems.

Kaitlyn, 8

Taylor, 6

105